The Armor of God

ISBN 979-8-88685-852-5 (paperback)
ISBN 979-8-89345-479-6 (hardcover)
ISBN 979-8-88685-853-2 (digital)

Christian Faith Publishing
832 Park Avenue
Meadville, PA 16335
www.christianfaithpublishing.com

All scriptures, unless otherwise stated, are taken from the Evangelical Heritage Version of the Holy Bible.

Printed in the United States of America

The Armor of God

Donna Hastreiter and Kathryn Nelson

"I'll save you, Mom!" Levi shouted as he burst through the door, brandishing his backpack and waving his pencil around like a sword.

"What's all this?" Mom asked, as Levi sneaked around the kitchen looking for danger.

"We learned about knights today and how they protected people from dragons and *everything*! I'll make sure you're safe!"

"We learned about kings and queens and princesses too," added Levi's twin sister, Mia, as she walked through the door. "I wish I could be a princess!"

"That *would* be nice," replied Mom. "It would make *me* a queen!"

Turning to Levi, she said, "I don't think you'll find anything dangerous around here, but maybe you two could help me attack this plate of cookies."

A chorus of happy shouts filled the kitchen. After devouring every last chocolate chip and telling Mom more about their day, the twins ran off to play.

A little while later, loud voices from the playroom filled Mom's ears and caused her to investigate. When she entered the playroom, she saw Levi and Mia pointing at each other and heard a chorus of "You ruined it!" "No, I didn't! It's your own fault!"

She looked past them to the pile of blocks scattered everywhere on the floor. "All right. Let's start at the beginning. Levi first."

"I made an awesome fortress, and my knights were invading it to battle the dragon when Mia came over and grabbed the leader right out of my hand! I tried to get it back, but she pushed me into the castle and it broke," Levi's words tumbled out.

"That's not true," Mia retorted. "I asked and asked for him to be quiet, but he kept being loud. I was trying to read my *Magic Princess Storytime* book, and I couldn't concentrate with all of his noise. I told him if he didn't stop, I'd take the knights away. It's not *my* fault he didn't listen."

Mom had Mia and Levi sit down next to her on the couch. "Do you remember anything that we read in the Bible about loving each other and getting along with each other?"

Mia glared at Levi. "I was trying! I asked him a hundred times to be quiet! How is it *my* fault when *he* doesn't listen? How can I get along with *him* when he doesn't cooperate with *me*?"

"Well," said Mom, "we can't do it on our own. Remember how we read that the Devil is like a roaring lion looking for someone to devour? The Devil was busy here today, tempting you both to sin and disobey God."

"Aha!" said Levi, pointing wildly at the ceiling. "So it's the Devil's fault!"

"No," answered Mom. "The Devil tempted you to sin, but you made the choice to follow his temptation. The Devil is very powerful and tricky."

"Then what are we supposed to do?" cried Mia, slumping down into her seat.

"Well, remember how you were telling me that you learned about knights at school today? How they had special equipment they used to fight dragons? Well, the Bible tells us that God gives us special weapons to fight the Devil."

"Really?" asked Levi, sitting up with more interest. "What are they?"

"We call the pieces the Armor of God. There are six different things we can use to protect ourselves from the Devil or help fight him off. Let's get our Bible and look in Ephesians, first at what we're fighting and then at what God gives us."

BIBLE

Levi scrambled over to get the Bible and bring it to Mom.

The twins leaned over her shoulders as she read Ephesians 6:10–16:

> Finally, be strong in the Lord and in his mighty power. Put on the full armor of God, so that you can stand against the schemes of the Devil. For our struggle is not against flesh and blood, but against the rulers, against the authorities, against the world rulers of this darkness, against the spiritual forces of evil in the heavenly places.

"Wow! What we're fighting against sounds really scary," exclaimed Mia.

"That's why we need God's help," replied Mom. "Because we can't fight on our own. Now let's look at the armor God gives us for protection." She continued reading in Ephesians 6:

For this reason, take up the full armor of God, so that you will be able to take a stand on the evil day and, after you have done everything, to stand. Stand, then, with the belt of truth buckled around your waist, with the breastplate of righteousness fastened in place, and with the readiness that comes from the gospel of peace tied to your feet like sandals. At all times hold up the shield of faith, with which you will be able to extinguish all the flaming arrows of the Evil One. Also take the helmet of salvation and the sword of the Spirit, which is the word of God.

Sword of the Spirit
Breastplate of Righteousness
Shield of Faith
Sandals of Peace
Helmet of Salvation
Belt of Truth

Mom looked up from the page. "That's a lot of armor, isn't it! Let's go over it one piece at a time. What do belts do?"

"They hold your pants up," Levi answered.

"They can also hold things—like Daddy's tools," added Mia.

"Right," replied Mom. "It's something you wrap around yourself to help prepare you for the day. When your belt is on, you don't have to worry about losing your pants—you're ready to go out and play. And when your dad has his tool belt on, he's ready to go off to work. We need the belt of truth wrapped around us to help prepare us to fight the Devil. What do you think the truth in the belt is?"

"Everything the Bible says!" Levi shouted eagerly, bouncing up onto his knees.

"That's right," Mom agreed. "We are reminded that we are children of God when we remember that Jesus lived, died, and rose to save us from our sins. That can give us courage when the Devil attacks. And when we wrap ourselves in God's truths, we're more prepared to identify the Devil's lies.

The Devil likes to lie and to twist God's words around. Remember when he tempted Eve in the garden or Jesus in the wilderness? He used little bits of God's Word to trick Eve and to try to trick Jesus. Eve relied on her own knowledge to fight back, instead of going back to God's truth. That's why she couldn't resist the Devil. Jesus knew all of God's Word and used those truths to recognize the lies so He wouldn't get tricked [Genesis 3, Matthew 4]. That's why the belt of truth is so important. We can use it to help recognize the Devil's lies."

"What's a breastplate?" asked Levi, pointing to the next part of the verse.

"That's a special piece of metal that knights used to wear to protect the front of their body, including their hearts. It's kind of like the bulletproof vests that policemen use today. The breastplate Paul is writing about is something called *righteousness*. That's a big word. It means 'right with God.' God isn't angry with us about our sins anymore because Jesus already paid for them. When we remember that truth, it makes it harder for the Devil to attack our hearts and steal our souls. He tries to pull us away from God, so we end up in Hell with him forever—his ultimate evil goal. When we cover ourselves with Jesus's righteousness, the Devil can't attack our heart or reach our soul."

Levi grabbed a pillow and held it to his chest. "Like this?" he asked.

"Exactly like that," replied Mom.

"Our feet should be fitted with the gospel of peace," she continued. "People use footwear, like shoes or sandals, to protect their feet. You use different kinds of shoes for different things, like dancing, hiking, or playing in the snow. The shoes we use for fighting the Devil are fitted with the gospel of peace. God wants us to live in peace with each other. That's one of the fruits of the Spirit you learned about in Sunday school. He also wants us to share the gospel of peace with others. Who knows what that is?"

"Jesus lived a perfect life, died for our sins, and rose again, and now we don't have to be afraid because of our sins. We have peace with God," Mia answered.

"Very good," said Mom. "That's another way to fight the Devil—telling other people the gospel so they can have peace with God.

ENVY
LIES
CHEAT
STEALING
KILL
VANITY
HATE
REASON
DESPAIR
Get well soon

Now, the Bible says that the Devil's temptations are like flaming arrows he shoots at us. What could we use to defend ourselves against that?"

"We'd need a shield, like the knights!" shouted Levi.

"That's the next thing in Paul's list," Mom replied, "the shield of faith. Faith means knowing, trusting, and following God's will—the things He tells us in the Bible. The bigger our faith is, the bigger our shield against the Devil will be. That's why it's so important to go to church and have devotions and read the Bible. The more you study God's Word, the stronger your faith becomes, and the bigger and stronger your shield against the Devil will be. And think about it. Would you rather fight an enemy with a little plastic shield or a big, strong, metal one?"

"The big one!" exclaimed Levi. "The biggest one in the world!"

"That's what I'd pick too." Mom grinned.

She pointed to the next piece of armor in the passage. "So far, you're protecting your heart and your feet. Another important thing to protect is your head. To protect your head, you need the helmet of salvation. *Salvation*, the word that means being saved by Jesus, is ours as a gift from God. The Devil can't take it away from us. He may try to get us to use our reason, or brain, to convince us that we are not good enough to go to Heaven or to doubt God's will or promises, but knowing and remembering our salvation will protect us from those spiritual 'arrows,' like a helmet protects our heads and brains from physical harm.

YOU'RE NOT GOOD ENOUGH
YOU CAN'T TRUST GOD
INRI

"In addition to the armor that protects us from the Devil's attacks, God has given us a weapon we can use to fight back. It's called the sword of the Spirit. Do you remember when the Devil tempted Jesus in the wilderness? What did Jesus do?"

"Every time the Devil tempted Him, Jesus used a Bible passage to fight back?" asked Mia.

"That's right!" said Mom. "And you know what? We have the same weapon Jesus did! When the Devil tempts you to be mean to each other, you can tell him to go away because God wants us to 'be kind one to another' [Ephesians 4:32] and tells us that 'we should love each other' [John 13:34–35]. The more Bible passages you know, the more weapons you have to use against the Devil!"

"I bet no one knows more Bible verses than Pastor," said Mia.

Mom smiled at her. "That might be true, but even he had to start somewhere. And even he needs to go back and review the ones he memorized a long time ago."

"Now, who can think of some ways the Devil tempts us and how it helps to know about the armor God gives us?"

"Well," Mia started, "when bad or sad things happen? Like when I broke my arm or when Grandma died?"

"Or when those big kids on the bus were being mean to me," interrupted Levi. "Stuff like that makes you think that nobody likes you or that God doesn't care about you."

"That's when we should remember the breastplate of righteousness and the helmet of salvation," said Mia. "If God loved us enough to send Jesus to make us right with Him and let us into Heaven, He will always love us and care for us, even if it seems like nobody else does."

"Very good!" Mom beamed.

WE LOVE YOU

Get
well soon

"Sometimes when I eat lunch at my friend's house and they don't pray first, I feel weird about praying by myself," Mia said. "I worry about what they might think."

"That would be a good time to remember the sandals of peace," said Levi. "If they ask what you're doing, you can tell them why you talk to God and tell them about Jesus and what He did for us. Then maybe they'll want to learn more about God and have peace with Him too."

"When else should we remember the sandals of peace?" Mom asked. After a very long pause, she added, "Think about earlier this afternoon."

Mia and Levi looked away. "We should remember that we should live in peace with each other when we're mad and want to fight with each other," Mia whispered.

"That's right," Mom said. "Now, can you think of how we can use the shield and sword God gives us?"

Levi spoke up, "The Devil sometimes tries to trick us into believing his lies—like we're not good enough to go to Heaven, or it's OK to be mean to somebody who was mean to us. We can use the shield of faith to block those lies, and we can use the sword of the Spirit to fight back with God's words."

"Great job, Levi!" exclaimed Mom. "And it's important to keep the shield and sword close at all times, so you're ready whenever the Devil tempts you. That's why it's so important to wrap ourselves in God's words with his belt of truth around us."

John 3:16
John 3:16
Hebrews 11:1
Romans 3:22-24
Hebrews 4:12
Hebrews 4:12
Romans 3:22-24
Hebrews 11:1
John 17:17
John 17:17
Ephesians 4:32
Ephesians 4:32
Ephesians 4:32
Ephesians 4:32

Get well soon

She pointed back to the Bible in her lap. "God actually gives us one last thing to help fight the Devil."

Levi frowned. "I didn't see anything else in that passage."

"It's in the next verse. In Ephesians 6:18, it says, 'At every opportunity, pray in the Spirit with every kind of prayer and petition.' God wants us to pray to Him for any and every reason—that includes asking Him for strength to fight the Devil and thanking Him for the armor He gave us."

Levi jumped up from the couch. "I'm ready for you now, Devil!" he shouted as he made slashing motions with his invisible sword. "Just try to get me!" he continued, ducking behind his invisible shield.

"I'm glad you're ready to use the armor God gave you," Mom said. "Just remember that you can't fight the Devil alone. You still need God's help. The Devil is real and will continue to tempt you and try to find cracks in your armor. You need to keep reading and hearing God's Word to keep your armor strong and in good shape, and you need to keep praying to God for help, because He is the only one more powerful than the Devil."

"OK, Mom," Levi said. "I'll try and remember. I'm sorry I kept making noise, Mia."

"I'm sorry I took your knight away," Mia replied. "Let's build another castle—like the one in my book. Then let's fight the dragon together!"

BIBLE

About the Authors

Donna Hastreiter has been a book lover all of her life. She enjoys spending time outside in her gardens, walking and biking with her husband, collecting antique books, and visiting her four adult children.

Kathryn Nelson is a nurse and avid reader who enjoys spending time with her husband and daughter. Together they have a menagerie of several frogs, two dogs, two turtles, and a cat.

www.ingramcontent.com/pod-product-compliance
Lightning Source LLC
Chambersburg PA
CBHW041819110726
48006CB00019B/2443